Special to God

Biblical Poetry for Family Worship

Wisdom from Grandma Series - Book 1

Grace Boucaud-Moore

Illustrated by Amanda Chureson
Edited by Genevieve Boucaud

Unless otherwise indicated, all Scripture quotations are taken from the King James Version. Public domain.

Scripture quotations marked NIV are taken from THE HOLY BIBLE, NEW INTERNATIONAL VERSION®, NIV® Copyright © 1973, 1978, 1984, 2011 by Biblica, Inc.® Used by permission. All rights reserved worldwide.

Copyright © 2023 Grace Boucaud-Moore
Copyright © 2023 TEACH Services, Inc.
ISBN-13: 978-1-4796-1571-1 (Paperback)
ISBN-13: 978-1-4796-1572-8 (ePub)
Library of Congress Control No: 2023909535

Acknowledgments

I say thanks to Roman Jabulani Shakeem Moore Henry who was the motivation for this writing project and to my daughter Alissa for sharing with me what reading together with her as a child meant to her.

Special thanks to my sister, Dr. Genevieve Boucaud, who first suggested that my writing might be publish-worthy, at a time when I was simply writing for my expected grandson. Her tremendous involvement as editor is evidenced by the poem 'Paradise Lost' which she penned and graciously allowed me to include to fill a gap in my storyline. Whereas my personal experience in writing these poems was highly emotional, Dr. Boucaud's editing work forced me to consider the accuracy of my expressed theology, as well as the needs of my unforeseen and unsuspecting audience.

I express my heartfelt thanks to Dr. Boucaud for her hours of wrestling with me, her contributions, and for being "the wind beneath my wings."

Thanks to all other supporters who added their encouragement as I continued writing, shared, and invited their reviews. Among them, Isiah Robley, was my most constant cheerleader.

I thank all my honest reviewers who though they saw some value in my work, were not so gullible as to pronounce it a perfect work.

Finally, I thank God who gifted me just enough to express my heart and not a bit more, and my dear readers who will graciously receive these poems as my way of sharing the good news that God has shared with me through Bible study.

Table of Contents

Special to God   4

Leadership   10

Helpmeet   12

Paradise Lost   14

Just Knowing God   16

God   19

Scripture Song   21

God's Plans   22

A Colossal Mistake   24

Love Made a Way   27

Why Build a Church?   30

A Special Book   34

A Special People   36

A Special Longing   38

Born Again!   40

Special to God

Six days God spent creating, the sun, the moon, the stars
The planets in the heavens, like Jupiter and Mars

God made a special planet; the planet we call Earth
He filled it with lots of animals, capable of giving birth

God prepared a special garden, with lots of fruit trees, tall and grand
The garden was to be the home for a special creature He called man

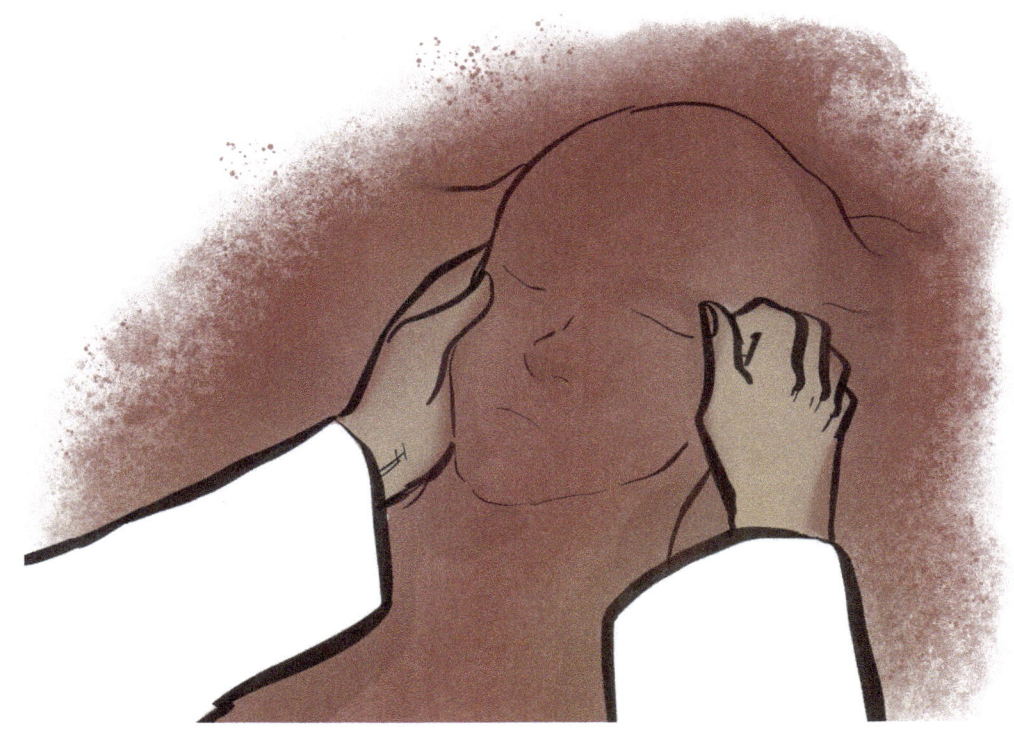

Man was not like any animal, nor was he like a tree
God declared, he must be special, "This one," He said, "will be like me."

"The man will share my wisdom, he will rule just like a king
The universe will see my ways, in the care he takes of things"

God named this being Adam; he was just as God desired
And He put him in the garden to tend it as required

Adam's first assignment was naming creatures, great and small
As this ceremony advanced, one fact was evident to all

Like God before creation, Adam felt yearning deep within
He longed for one just like him, a helpmeet, a wife, kin

It was God's intent to provide him a helpmeet all along
And so, Adam gazed upon her, on his lips a blissful song

"Bone of my bone, flesh of my flesh, taken out of man"
And the Father beamed content at the unveiling of His plan

For in their love for each other, one mind, one flesh, one bone
Was the image of His Father; they were their Father's own

(see Gen. 1–2)

Leadership

God made Adam, tall and strong,
Why, he could work all the day long;
God also made him good and kind,
Steadfast, true in heart and mind.

As husband, and as father too,
Adam would know just what to do.
Chosen to protect and serve,
His family would have all they deserved.

Engaging each one heart to heart,
Adam would faithfully do his part;
Teaching always the one true creed,
While providing for his family's needs.

As each one felt safe, valued, and loved,
They'd all declare to heaven above:
"God is good, and we are blest,
As Adam's love and care attest."

So Adam would bear witness true
Painting life in colourful hue
As his Father had done before
And one could not desire more.

Helpmeet

God gave to Adam a helper one day,
She was to help him consider the way;
To leave Adam alone was not thought to be good,
For things to develop as God planned that they should.

As helper, Eve would surely put Adam first,
Without her help, they could invite a curse;
But God desired for Adam a life fully blest,
With Eve, and the Father, he could ace any test.

The heart of her husband was safe in her care,
Bound in the Father's and the love that they shared;
And she certainly had a firm will to do,
Whatsoever was right and whatever was true.

Like her Father, Eve was gracious and kind,
She possessed a pure heart and Christ-like mind;
She was also venturesome, brave and strong,
Committed and knowing to whom she belonged.

As for God, He ensured Eve had every provision,
To stand by her husband with ne'er a division;
And so it was that God's plan was set,
With full trust in the Father, there'd be no regret.

Paradise Lost

All of nature was lovely in the garden made for man
It was in this perfect garden that Earth's story first began
And 'twas also here in this happy home where Adam lived with Eve
Evil suddenly entered in a manner hard to believe.

The jewelled sky was glorious, the moon, the stars, the sun
And animals grazed happily; life was peaceful, joyous, fun
Graceful giraffes, funny monkeys, every animal a friend
It was here that evil entered, though it's hard to comprehend.

The fruit trees were all laden, oh what succulent delight!
Their colours, like the flowers, in subtle hues and bright
Everything was perfect, precisely as God planned
How evil found a place there is hard to understand.

One day while in the garden, Eve met the enemy of God
Known as the father of all lies, a deceiver and a fraud
He wove his lies around her; she didn't run or flee
So 'twas here that evil entered underneath a tree.

He told her things about God that were evil and untrue
"You can be wise," he told her, "here's what you should do."
"Forget your Father. Eat this fruit. You'll know more than you now know."
Eve ate and evil entered, and then it began to grow.

Eve then turned to Adam and said "Try this. It is good."
And Adam, too, ate of the fruit knowing that he never should
And suddenly paradise was lost, the beauty God had made
For it was in this paradise that they first disobeyed.

And the formerly happy couple now knew sorrow, shame, and fear
And hid from the Father as their predicament became clear
For surely now they understood they'd have to pay the cost
Though little did they realise that paradise was lost.

Just Knowing God

You, too, were made by God above,
Because He wants to share His love;
For though He has an enemy,
He is able to protect you completely.

He knows the danger; He sees the threat,
But for His plan has no regret;
Since He is omniscient and wise,
Sin would come as no surprise.

And though infallible you are not,
He aims to bless you with all He's got;
God sees a lot of promise in you,
You may yet attest to what is true.

Knowing Him will give you strength,
You are sure to overcome at length;
Just strive to understand His will
And find in Him your greatest thrill.

Submit to God; resist the foe,
Show God's love where'er you go.
And you'll be safe, and you'll be blessed
And you will have His peace and rest.

"O LORD, our Lord, how excellent is thy name in all the earth! who hast set thy glory above the heavens. Out of the mouth of babes and sucklings hast thou ordained strength because of thine enemies, that thou mightest still the enemy and the avenger"
(Ps. 8:1, 2).

"...And Jesus saith unto them, Yea; have ye never read, Out of the mouth of babes and sucklings thou hast perfected praise?"
(Matt. 21:16).

God

You will not see Him with your eyes,
Listening ears will not hear Him much;
God is such a grand surprise,
You will not know Him by your touch.

But you can see the things He made,
You will discover noises, too;
And if you knew the plans He laid,
You'd be convinced that He loves you.

The book of nature shows it plain,
That God is good, His comforts real;
And in His letters, this glad refrain,
Jesus saves and Jesus heals.

Have you been hurt?
Do you know fear?
Then open your heart,
He'll meet you there.

(see Job 11:7, 8; Acts 17:24–27)

Scripture Song

Search me, O God, and know my heart today,
Try me, O Saviour, know my thoughts, I pray;
See if there be, some wicked way in me;
Cleanse me from every sin, and set me free.

Search me, O God, and know my heart today,
Try me, O Saviour, know my thoughts, I pray;
Listen if there be, some wicked way in me;
Cleanse me from every sin, and set me free.

Lord, take my life, and make it wholly thine,
Fill my poor heart with Thy great love divine;
Take all my will, my passion, self, and pride;
I now surrender, Lord, in me abide. (repeat line)

Orr, J. Edwin. "Search Me, O God." Hymnary. Accessed January 23, 2023. https://hymnary.org/text/search_me_o_god_and_know_my_heart_orr.

God's Plans

God lays His plans so carefully,
Preparing for any possibility.
Nothing takes Him by surprise,
Eternity is stretched out before His eyes.

He knew you long before your birth
And where you'd be while here on earth
He has big dreams, and He will do
Great and marvellous things for you.

God loves you deeply; I hope you know,
Through all the years He will watch you grow;
His eyes search always to and fro
To guide and bless you here below.

He made you special; this is true
With paths to walk and tasks to do
He's given you talents to meet those tasks
If you but knock and seek and ask.

Rely on Him; give Him your heart
Commit yourself to walk His path
And though you may sometimes go astray,
He can redeem you to obey.

The choice is yours, His will to fulfil,
Let His way be your greatest thrill;
You may become a leader grand,
If you choose to heed the Master's plan.

A Colossal Mistake

Adam and Eve were sore afraid,
A colossal mistake they had made;
And God, their best and truest friend,
Was sure to find out in the end.

They made garments of fig leaves,
To cover their nakedness whilst they grieved;
The loss that they sustained was great,
And strangely their hearts were filled with hate.

Eve blamed the serpent; Adam blamed Eve,
Lucifer was glad, would you believe,
The blame, he placed upon the Son,
Because of the wondrous things He'd done?

"Wasn't it God who had made man?
Didn't He conceive a master plan?
Wasn't the man to rule the earth?
And to acclaim the Creator's worth?"

But in as much as this was all past,
That devil thought he'd have his dream at last—
His own subjects, kingdom, royal acclaim,
And the utter ruin of God's name.

Alas, alas, God's work was undone!
Would He concede? Had Satan won?
Had this taken the Father all by surprise?
Certainly not! For our God is wise.

Love Made a Way

Long ago, the sad story goes, man fallen from grace,
Legally lost divine favour, as well as his place;
Sentenced to death for embracing a lie,
He could no longer go to his Father on high.

The sorrow of God, none could fully know,
Though the angels of heaven attest it was a harsh blow;
That the children of men fell under a curse,
And to ignore their condition, well, that would be worse.

Not one of them could deliver the other; they were fully lost
Not father, nor mother, nor brother could pay redemption's cost
An outsider was needed to enter the race,
To bring to mankind salvation through grace.

The very best angel couldn't suffice to restore divine favour
Though good and kind, no angel would claim to be the Life-giver;
But the Father had ordained a definitive plan
Jesus, God's Son, would be sent to save man.

As one of the family, by giving His life He would bring salvation,
A ransom for all, He would restore man's rightful station.
For promised to each who would trust in this Son,
Was new birth and life with the resurrected One.

As promised to mankind, the Saviour came, He lived and then He died,
He showed us the truth, and how to live and in Him abide;
And gave us the Spirit, as our Comforter and Friend,
And so, His great love sustains us secure to the end.

So, long ago, as the story goes, God's love found a way,
To forgive, cleanse and restore us, and empower us to obey;
And I am happy that God has showed us His plan,
To restore the relationship between God and man.

Why Build a Church?

My God is never arbitrary
He has a reason for each plan
His projects are well thought-out
His reason is never merely 'cause He can!

His work is based on principles
Those are laws that never change
But circumstances, they may alter
And His procedures rearrange

When I fail or make a mistake
My procedure, too, needs a shift
But though God's way is always perfect
His nature is to give others a lift

Before Jesus left earth for heaven
He wanted to build us a church
He had a really good reason—
He would not leave us in a lurch

Jesus, you know, is the God-man
And we all know that God is good
This very principle tells us
Build a strong church, He should

How could Jesus secure all His children?
For Christ, it was plain to see
What was needed was true brotherhood
Born of a genuine Christianity

Christ-mindedness in all its members
Makes us each a lover of truth
To the Word we go in each conflict
So none would despise even the youth

It matters not that in His body
I may be a foot, an ear, or a hand
I know that Christ is the head
And my feelings, He understands

He has given me a place in His body
Because I must also be and do
The complete will of my Master
In fulfilling His mission too

Judiciously, Christ has given each member
A distinctive vote and voice
In matters of making decisions
We each must affirm God's choice

In applying my will to these matters
God intends that I will be made strong
He means I must grow in His wisdom
So as to be like Him afore long

The wheat and tares may grow together
But God's children need know no fear
Because He has smartly equipped us
His truth principles to share

Values that reflect God's character
All of them, described in His Word
Form and reshape all His children
To keep law through the Spirit of God

The church is comprised of God's people
On them He bestows great regard
If faithful, all these special children
Will receive the eternal reward

A Special Book

Baby books, photo albums, journals, and diaries
Letters, autographs, memoirs, and biographies
Milestones and memories of loves and journeys taken
Their real value found in the joy they re-awaken

God has His books of remembrance, as well
Of His engagements with us and pleasures they tell
Records of identity, works, tears, new births
Yet the Bible, by far, exceeds all these in worth

Why, you may ask, have I reached this conclusion?
I give you my word, there'll soon be no confusion.
You see, surely God knows we have suffered great loss
Separation anxiety brings phenomenal cost

The Bible shows us that God is still near
That, for us, He continues deeply to care
Although we can't see Him or talk face-to-face
This Good Book portrays His continuous grace

Our God speaks comfort to us in this way
And if we but listen to what He has to say
He'll give us guidance to continue learning
To share in His wisdom and be more discerning

The truths of the Word debunk lies we've been told
That have lain in our hearts and brought ruin to souls
Manufacturing sadness, hate, selfishness, lust
Quenching godly impulses like faith, hope, and trust

His words, they are active and work transformation
Together with His Spirit to bring us salvation
They probe the real motives oft concealed in our hearts
Leading us to repent and from sin to depart

And He has sent you this Book so that you might see
That He is interested in you personally
Revealing His love and His principles fair
And counsels that cry out, Beware! Beware!

So as you journey homeward, please treasure this Book
Discover for yourself the great pains our God took
To guide you to the joyous home that awaits
And the arms of the Saviour just beyond heaven's gates.

A Special People

What makes God's people special?
I'm convinced, it's their integrity
They practice godly principles
Not the way we are inclined to be

Special people are true believers
In the supreme God above
They depend on Him in all things
And rightly value His love

To the saints, God's word is infallible
And since He makes no mistakes
They trust only one way to be saved
And obey Him for their own souls' sakes

As God is both good and consistent
So Christians also strive to be
United in mission and service
Heeding His call to ordered ministry

Christians honour the headship of Jesus
And cherish their own brotherhood
They invite the infilling of the Spirit
Who makes them productive of good

Special disciples are unlike the Gentiles
Amongst them, there are no overlords
For any who aspire to greatness
First, must be a servant of all

God's church was created a safe place
A true haven and refuge from sin
Like the ark long ago He ordained it
To gather His people to Him

A Special Longing

My Saviour made me a promise,
A promise long ago,
That I need never feel rejected,
As I travel here below.

Though the sting of earth's great trials,
Reminds me I've made sore mistakes,
He gives me His constant assurance,
His promises He will never break.

I reflect on my soul's aching hunger,
I feel the bitterest thirst,
I think of the sweet, promised manna,
And the tree I will ever put first.

The knowledge of good and evil,
The things Satan promised to me,
Have not made good on their promise,
So, I long for the life-giving tree.

Life can become so weary.
Oh! The nakedness, conflict, and lies!
But my Saviour has made me a promise:
No more heartaches, no tears, no goodbyes.

My Father will give me new garments,
A crown and a seat on His throne,
Why! He will even give me a new name
That will be written upon a white stone.

My Father has made me a promise,
A promise I know to be sure
That I need never feel rejected
I have a room in His home evermore.

"And I will put enmity between thee and the woman, and between thy seed and her seed; it shall bruise thy head, and thou shalt bruise his heel" (Gen. 3:15).

"Jesus answered, "I am the **way** and the **truth** and the **life**. No one comes to the Father except through me" (John 14:6, NIV, emphasis added).

Born Again!

Ancestry? Roots? Heritage? What did they bequeath to me?
The image of God birthed in Eden or human depravity?
According to the great king, David, a man after God's own heart,
Entrenched in sin and degeneracy was where he got his start.

Solomon, the wisest of all the kings, has also made it quite plain,
The foolishness found in the heart of each child; all parents must restrain.
My Jesus, though, is quite hopeful that with trust and humility,
Righteousness, discipline, and peacefulness He can produce in me.

Like He said to Nicodemus, the Pharisee who went to Him one night
And wished to be a Christian, but just could not get it right,
The knowledge of the law and the promise could not free him from blame
No, to be a part of God's kingdom, "Ye must be born again!"

He meant we should be filled with the Spirit to help us God's ways to keep
And for this I must do the inviting; "Holy Spirit, make, please make me God's sheep.
Cleanse my heart of every defilement; energize me for your service sweet.
Give me wisdom for faithful fruit-bearing, give me victory in every feat."

Like Enoch, I long to walk faithful to every command of my Lord
And hear His voice, as to Abraham, declare me a friend of my God
"Holy Spirit, mould me in God's image, cleanse my soul from every stain
Take my heart, for I cannot give it. Help me now to be born again."

(see John 3:7)

TEACH Services, Inc.
PUBLISHING

We invite you to view the complete
selection of titles we publish at:
www.TEACHServices.com

We encourage you to write us
with your thoughts about this,
or any other book we publish at:
info@TEACHServices.com

TEACH Services' titles may be purchased in
bulk quantities for educational, fund-raising,
business, or promotional use.
bulksales@TEACHServices.com

Finally, if you are interested in seeing
your own book in print, please contact us at:
publishing@TEACHServices.com

We are happy to review your manuscript at no charge.